Śrī Śrī Premadhāma-Deva-Stotram

Golden Gift of the Golden Lord

Śrī Śrī Premadhāma-Deva-Stotram

Golden Gift of the Golden Lord

Swāmī B.R. Śrīdhara

MANDALA
PUBLISHING

For philosophical inquiries please contact:

SRI NARASINGHA CAITANYA MATHA
P.O. Box 21, Sri Rangapatna - Karnataka-571 438, India
E-mail: gosai@gosai.com
Web site: http://www.gosai.com/chaitanya/
or
SRI CAITANYA SARASVATA MATHA
Kolerganj, P.O. Navadvipa, Dist. Nadia, West Bengal, 741302 India

SENIOR EDITORS:
Tridaṇḍī Gosvāmī Śrī Śrīpāda
Bhakti Gaurava Narasiṅgha Mahārāja
and
Tridaṇḍī Gosvāmī Śrī Śrīpāda
Bhakti Bhāvana Viṣṇu Mahārāja

ASSISTED BY NUMEROUS EVER-ASPIRING SERVANTS
OR SRI SRI GURU AND GAURANGA

To order this and other books by
Gosai Publishers and Mandala Publishing Group contact:

MANDALA PUBLISHING GROUP
354 Bel Marin Keys Blvd. Suite D, Novato, CA 94949 USA
e-mail: mandala@mandala.org
website: www.mandala.org
phone: 415.883.4055
fax: 415.884.0500
orders: 800.688.2218

First printing: 2002 limited edition 1,000 copies

Printed in China through Palace Press International

ISBN: 1-886069-06-9

His Divine Grace
Srila Bhakti Raksaka Sridhara Deva Goswami Maharaja
The illustrious Author

His Divine Grace
Srila Bhaktisiddhanta Saraswati Goswami Thakura Prabhupada

Sri Caitanya Sarasvata Matha

Lord Nityananda Prabhu

Lord Caitanya Mahaprabhu

All glories, all glories
unto my golden Lord Gaurasundara
the beautiful, the divine abode
of pure love. Demigods, mystics,
salvationists, yogīs and pure devotees
of Lord Kṛṣṇa—all sing constantly
in His praise.

Introduction

In the 15th century a mysterious, divine personality appeared on earth in West Bengal, India. His name was Śrī Caitanya. He had extremely beautiful features and a most unusual golden effulgence. Many of His devotees fondly called Him 'Gaurasundara' (beautiful golden one) and 'Gaurāṅga' (one whose complexion resembles molten gold). His heart was full of devotional love for the Supreme Divine Truth Kṛṣṇa and compassion for all living beings. Pious people who came in contact with Him could not but deeply revere and love Him. They believed through realization that He was the non-different manifestation of the Supreme Divinity and the embodiment of divine love-ecstasy. During Śrī Gaurāṅga's manifest presence and after, some of His pure devotees composed beautiful devotional songs about Him expressing their profound love and appreciation. This *Prema Dhāma Deva Stotram* is one of them — a uniquely excellent treasure of *Gaura-līlā*, imbued with the innate beauty of the author's own *Gaura-prema*. Fondly addressing Śrī Gaurāṅga as *prema-dhāma-deva* (the Lord, who is the unlimited abode of divine love), he eloquently describes His transcendental life and precepts.

In the higher stage of devotional realization, the pastimes or activities of a dearly worshipable divine personality are fully experienced and understood in a most extraordinary way. Through the power of their pure dedication and unwavering love, pure devotees experience the transcendental nature of *Gaura-līlā* whether on the plane of eternity (*nitya-līlā*) or the earthly plane including its apparently ordinary activities (*bhauma-līlā*). This holy composition is a vivid example of this. Deeply inspired by his guru Śrīla Sarasvatī Ṭhākura, the author dove deep into the nectar ocean of *Gaura-līlā* and instantly experienced its divine beauty and taste. Having discovered the transcendental world of ecstatic love of Gaura as revealed by great devotees such as Śrī Rūpa, Raghunātha and Kavirāja Gosvāmī, he could not but feel deeply influenced and charmed as he experienced the wonderful surging waves of *Gaura-prema* throughout his inner existence. Most eager to express his profound love and admiration for Śrī Gaurāṅga, he gradually began to compose a series of poems in glorification of his worshipable beloved. In due course of time, that sweet desire was fulfilled with the completion of this beautiful *stotra*.

This composition is based on the *Caitanya-caritāmṛta* and other authentic writings about Śrī Gaurāṅga. It describes Him as Śrī Kṛṣṇa, the Supreme Personality of Divine Truth, permeated with the mood (*bhāva*) and complexion (*kānti*) of His pleasure potency, Śrī Rādhikā. It reveals Śrī Gaurāṅga as the personification of the unlimited ocean of ecstatic love of Kṛṣṇa as experienced by Śrī Rādhikā. It also shows how He was a kind philanthropist who gave that *Kṛṣṇa-prema* in charity to His devotees.

It also presents His major life's activities, characteristics, qualities and conclusive principles in a summarized but beautifully interwoven way. Śrīla Advaita Ācārya's earnest prayer to invoke His appearance, His divine birth, His form of beauty, His playful childhood, His educational pastimes, His undefeatable expertise in raising and resolving the most sophisticated logical arguments with their harmonious conclusions, His unparalleled outstanding scholarship and wisdom, His love for Kṛṣṇa expressed through Kṛṣṇa *nāma-kīrtana*, His *sannyāsa* pastimes, His teachings to Śrī Rūpa and Sanātana, His tour of South India, His deeply meaningful talks with Rāya Rāmānanda and the revelation of His *svarūpa* as *rasarāja* and *mahābhāva*, His power in defeating the *māyāvāda* philosophy and establishing *acintya-bhedābheda-siddhānta*, His passage through Jhāḍikhaṇḍa on the way to Vṛndāvana, His wonderful excursions in the land of Vraja, His profound revelation of *Śikṣāṣṭakam*, His *rasāsvādana* (deep absorption in tasting the mellows of Rādhikā's love in separation from Kṛṣṇa) at Nīlācala in the intimate company of Śrī Svarūpa and Rāmānanda, His wandering along the ocean beach driven by the maddening waves of ambrosial pain of *Kṛṣṇa-prema*—are all described here in a sweet harmonious style.

This *stotra* also describes some of the most predominant aspects of Śrī Gaurāṅga's divine personality—His transcendental characteristics (*aprākṛta-vaiśiṣṭa*), qualities (*guṇa*), beauty (*rūpa*), charm (*ākarṣaṇa*), compassion (*karuṇā*), generosity (*audārya*), power (*tejas*), forgiving nature (*kṣamā-śīlatā*), magnanimity (*mahattva*), wisdom (*prajñāna*), conviction (*viśvāsa*), determination (*dṛḍha-saṅkalpatā*), self-contentment in ecstatic love for Kṛṣṇa (*svānubhāvānanda*), all-encompassing kind love for others (*sarva-jīve dayā*), limitless ecstatic love for Kṛṣṇa (*kṛṣṇa-prema-dhāma-rūpa*) and lastly His compassionate sharing of that divine love ecstasy with others (*mahā-vadānya-kṛṣṇa-prema-pradātṛtva*).

The ecstatic divine nature of Śrī Gaurāṅga's loving relationships with some of His dearmost devotees such as Śacī Mātā, Jagannātha Miśra, Lakṣmīpriyā, Viṣṇupriyā, Śrī Advaita, Śrī Nityānanda, Śrī Gadādhara Paṇḍita, Śrīvāsa Paṇḍita, Śrī Sārvabhauma, Rāja Pratāparudra, Śrī Rūpa, Śrī Sanātana, Śrī Raghunātha, Śrī Svarūpa and Śrī Rāmānanda and their intense love for Him was specifically relished by the author. He found his love for Śrī Gaurāṅga was enhanced by such devotion and therefore fondly describes, in brief, some of their different loving pastimes.

This *stotra* further describes how Śrī Gaurāṅga explained extremely difficult and sophisticated philosophical truths with perfect reasoning, disregarding the imperfect impersonal goals of the Māyāvādīs and established the excellence of attaining a beautiful life of devotional love engagement with Kṛṣṇa in His ecstatic pastimes (*cid-vilāsa*). He revealed the self-effulgent truth of His beautifully mysterious but self-evident conclusive philosophy of inconceivable, simultaneous oneness and distinction between Kṛṣṇa (*śaktimān*) and His different potencies (*śakti*) known as *acintya-bhedābheda-siddhānta.*

The author has composed this *stotra* using the Sanskrit *tūṇaka* meter which represents the dancing rhythm of spiritual delight. Such ecstatic dance was a prominent characteristic of Śrī Gaurāṅga's life and therefore the author felt especially inspired to choose this meter which has also been used by Śrī Rūpa Gosvāmī and Kavirāja Gosvāmī in some of their writings.

Another literary characteristic of this composition is its unique charming style which has created a wonderful harmony between its aesthetic poetic beauty and philosophical depth. It reminds the reader of the same special taste found in the disciplic line of Svarūpa Dāmodara, Rāmānanda, Rūpa, Raghunātha, Jīva and Kavirāja Gosvāmī, whose writings about Śrī Gaurāṅga captivate the mind and heart. It can thus be considered one of the most valuable contributions to the world of Gaura-Sarasvata literatures.

The underlying nectarine flow of this *stotra* is the author's sublime love for Śrī Gaurāṅga manifested in variegated mellows. Kavirāja Gosvāmī has beautifully described this type of realization in the following verse from his *Caitanya-caritāmṛta*:

kṛṣṇa-līlā amṛta-sāra, tāra śata śata dhāra
daśa-dike bahe yāhā haite
se caitanya-līlā haya, sarovara akṣaya
mano-haṁsa carāha tāhāte

The pastimes of Kṛṣṇa are the quintessence of all divine nectar and *Caitanya-līlā* is an inexhaustible lake of that nectar which, flowing in hundreds of streams, floods the hearts of the devotees from all directions. Therefore O nectar-seeking friend please let your mind swim in that lake like a regal swan. (Cc. 2.25.271)

Thus, in conclusion, we can know that the beloved author of this *stotra*, Śrīla Bhakti Rakṣaka Śrīdhara Deva Gosvāmī Mahārāja, certainly swam in that nectar ocean of *Caitanya-līlā* and invited all other nectar-seeking devotees to share this blissful experience.

The Verses

Verse 1

देवसिद्धमुक्तयुक्तभक्तवृन्दवन्दितं
पापतापदावदाहदग्धदुःखखण्डितम् ।
कृष्णनामसीधुधामधन्यदानसागरं
प्रेमधामदेवमेव नौमि गौरसुन्दरम् ॥१॥

deva-siddha-mukta-yukta-bhakta-vṛnda-vanditaṁ
pāpa-tāpa-dāva-dāha-dagdha-duḥkha-khaṇḍitam
kṛṣṇa-nāma-sīdhu-dhāma-dhanya-dāna-sāgaraṁ
prema-dhāma-devam eva naumi gaurasundaram

Translation

All glories, all glories unto my golden Lord Gaurasundara the beautiful, the divine abode of pure love. Demigods, mystics, salvationists, *yogīs* and pure devotees of Lord Kṛṣṇa—all sing constantly in His praise. He removes at once the miseries of all tortured souls who are scorched by the heat of their own sins and consequently are burning incessantly within the great forest fire of the material world. Blessed is the Lord who is a vast ocean of divine generosity, the abode of the sweet nectars that are the Holy Names of Kṛṣṇa.

VERSE 2

स्वर्णकोटिदर्पणाभदेहवर्णगौरवं
पद्मपारिजातगन्धवन्दिताङ्गसौरभम् ।
कोटिकाममूर्च्छिताङ्घ्रिरूपरासरङ्गरं
प्रेमधाममदेवमेव नौमि गौरसुन्दरम् ॥२॥

svarṇa-koṭi-darpaṇābha-deha-varṇa-gauravaṁ
padma-pārijāta-gandha-vanditāṅga-saurabham
koṭi-kāma-mūrcchitāṅghri-rūpa-rāsa-raṅgaraṁ
prema-dhāma-devam eva naumi gaurasundaram

TRANSLATION

The luster of His fair body is brighter than a million brilliant mirrors of gold. Of such sweetness is the fragrance of His body that the aromatic lotus and *pārijāta* flowers humbly offer their prayers of worship. Millions of Cupids, shocked out of their pride, swoon at His lotus feet, unable to bear the sight of His unparalleled beauty. His limbs are alive *rāsa* moods of love that emerge and flow continuously from His beautiful form. I sing with joy the unending glories of my sweet Lord, my golden Gaurasundara, the one and only divine abode of pure love.

VERSE 3

प्रेमनामदानजन्यपञ्चतत्त्वकात्मकं
साङ्गदिव्यपार्षदास्त्रवैभवावतारकम् ।
श्यामगौरनामगाननृत्यमत्तनागरं
प्रेमधाममदेवमेव नौमि गौरसुन्दरम् ॥३॥

prema-nāma-dāna-janya-pañca-tattvakātmakaṁ
sāṅga-divya-pārṣadāstra-vaibhavāvatārakam

śyāma-gaura-nāma-gāna-nṛtya-matta-nāgaraṁ
prema-dhāma-devam eva naumi gaurasundaram

Translation

He expanded Himself as the five-fold potencies of the Pañca-tattva in order to expedite the free distribution of the Holy Names of Kṛṣṇa leading to the attainment of *Kṛṣṇa-prema*, the fifth end. Fully equipped with His transcendental limbs and divine weapons and accompanied by His associates, He descended on earth in all His opulence. Being the Supreme Lord Śyāmasundara Himself, He appeared as Gaurasundara, dancing and singing the Holy Names in ecstasy through the streets of Nadīyā like an ordinary citizen. I sing with joy the unending glories of my golden Gaurasundara, my sweet Lord, the one and only divine abode of pure love.

Verse 4

शान्तिपूर्यधीशकल्यधर्म्मदुःखदुःसहं
जीवदुःखहानभक्तसौख्यदानविग्रहम् ।
कल्यघौघनाशकृष्णनामसीधुसञ्चरं
प्रेमधामदेवमेव नौमि गौरसुन्दरम् ॥४॥

śānti-puryadhīśa-kalyadharma-duḥkha-duḥsahaṁ
jīva-duḥkha-hāna-bhakta-saukhyadāna-vigraham
kalyaghaugha-nāśa-kṛṣṇa-nāma-sīdhu-sañcaraṁ
prema-dhāma-devam eva naumi gaurasundaram

Translation

He could not bear to see His devotee Advaita Prabhu, Lord of Śāntipura, in misery over the pitiable condition of the Kali-yuga which has been overtaken by irreligious philosophies. He therefore appeared in such a *vigraha* form in order to relieve the *jīva* from his misery, award happiness to His devotee, and to destroy the venom of Kali by profusely distributing the nectar of Kṛṣṇa's Names. I sing with joy the unending glories of my golden Gaurasundara the beautiful, the one and only divine abode of pure love.

VERSE 5

द्वीपनव्यगाङ्गबङ्गजन्मकर्म्मदर्शितं
श्रीनिवासवासधन्यनामरासहर्षितम् ।
श्रीहरिप्रियेशपूज्यधीशचीपुरन्दरं
प्रेमधामदेवमेव नौमि गौरसुन्दरम् ॥५॥

dvīpa-navya-gāṅga-baṅga-janma-karma-darśitaṁ
śrīnivāsa-vāsa-dhanya-nāma-rāsa-harṣitam
śrī haripriyeśa-pūjyadhī-śacī-purandaraṁ
prema-dhāma-devam eva naumi gaurasundaram

TRANSLATION

His divine birth and pastimes took place at Śrī Navadvīpa, on the banks of the holy Gaṅgā. He blessed the house of Śrīnivāsa (Śrīvāsa-aṅgana) filling the hearts of all with the blissful transcendental mellows of the Holy Name. He dutifully respected and adored His mother Śacī Devī and learned father Śrī Miśra; and to His wives Śrī Lakṣmīpriyā and Śrī Viṣṇupriyā, He was the Lord of their lives. I sing with joy the unending glories of Gaurasundara the beautiful, my golden Lord, the one and only divine abode of pure love.

VERSE 6

श्रीशचीदुलालबाल्यबालसङ्गचञ्चलं
आकुमारसर्वशास्त्रदक्षतर्कमङ्गलम् ।
छात्रसङ्गरङ्गदिग्जिगीषुदर्पसंहरं
प्रेमधामदेवमेव नौमि गौरसुन्दरम् ॥६॥

śrī-śacī-dulāla-bālya-bāla-saṅga-cañcalaṁ
ākumāra-sarva-śāstra-dakṣa-tarka-maṅgalam
chātra-saṅga-raṅga-digjigīṣu-darpa-saṁharaṁ
prema-dhāma-devam eva naumi gaurasundaram

TRANSLATION

As the son of Śacī Devī, He enjoyed mischievous childhood pastimes with other boys. As a mere youth He acquired mastery over all scriptures and by His expertise in the current method of logic He established the auspicious path of devotion for the welfare of all. On the banks of the Gaṅgā in the company of His students He vanquished the pride of the famous *digvijayī paṇḍita.* I sing with joy the unending glories of my golden Gaurasundara, the Lord of beauty, the one and only abode of divine love.

VERSE 7

वर्ज्यपात्रसारमेयसर्पसङ्गखेलनं
स्कन्धवाहिचौरतीर्थविप्रचित्रलीलनम् ।
कृष्णनाममात्रबाल्यकोपशान्तिसौकरं
प्रेमधामदेवमेव नौमि गौरसुन्दरम् ॥७॥

varjya-pātra-sārameya-sarpa-saṅga-khelanaṁ
skandha-vāhi-caura-tīrtha-vipra-citra-līlanam
kṛṣṇa-nāma-mātra-bālya-kopa-śānti saukaraṁ
prema-dhāma-devam eva naumi gaura-sundaram

TRANSLATION

His childhood pastimes were most wonderful. He used to play merrily with rejected utensils and inauspicious animals like pups and poisonous snakes. He was once carried away by a thief who wanted to steal His clothes. He appeared before the *tīrtha-vipra* (a *brāhmaṇa* who was constantly visiting the holy places of pilgrimage), and blessed him with His remnants. When He would cry in frustration, only the utterance of the Names of Kṛṣṇa would at once pacify Him. I sing with joy the unending glories of my golden Gaurasundara, my sweet Lord, the one and only divine abode of love.

VERSE 8

स्नानगाङ्गवारिबालसङ्गरङ्गखेलनं
बालिकादिपारिहास्यभङ्गिबाल्यलीलनम् ।
कूटतर्कछात्रशिक्षकादिवादतत्परं
प्रेमधामदेवमेव नौमि गौरसुन्दरम् ॥८॥

snāṇā-gāṅga-vāri-bāla-saṅga-raṅga-khelanaṁ
bālikādi-pārihāsya-bhaṅgi-bālya-līlanam
kūṭa-tarka-chātra-śikṣakādi-vāda-tatparaṁ
prema-dhāma-devam eva naumi gaurasundaram

TRANSLATION

He would play wonderfully in a variety of ways with His boyhood friends while bathing in the waters of the Gaṅgā. Sometimes in a jovial mood He would speak sweetly with the young girls as if teasing them. He would present complicated arguments and counter-arguments before His puzzled students and teachers. I sing with joy the unending glories of my golden Gaurasundara, my sweet Lord, the one and only divine abode of pure love.

VERSE 9

श्रीनिमाइपण्डितेतिनामदेशवन्दितं
नव्यतर्कदक्षलक्षदम्भिदम्भखण्डितम् ।
स्थापितार्थखण्डखण्डखण्डितार्थसम्भरं
प्रेमधामदेवमेव नौमि गौरसुन्दरम् ॥९॥

śrī nimāi-paṇḍiteti-nāma-deśa-vanditaṁ
navya-tarka-dakṣa-lakṣa-dambhi-dambha-khaṇḍitam
sthāpitārtha-khaṇḍa-khaṇḍa-khaṇḍitārtha-sambharaṁ
prema-dhāma-devam eva naumi gaurasundaram

TRANSLATION

He was respected all over the land as the learned scholar Nimāi Paṇḍita. He would crush the ego of the proud Nyāya scholars of His time by His numerous, ingenious and original arguments and after having thus shattered their traditional theories, He would again establish them. I sing with joy the unending glories of my golden Gaurasundara, Lord of my heart, the one and only abode of divine love.

VERSE 10

श्लोकगाङ्गवन्दनार्थदिग्जिगीषुभाषितं
व्यत्यलङ्कृतादिदोषतर्कितार्थदूषितम् ।

ध्वस्तयुक्तिरुद्धबुद्धिदत्तधीमदादरं
प्रेमधामदेवमेव नौमि गौरसुन्दरम् ॥१०॥

śloka-gāṅga-vandanārtha-digjigīṣu-bhāṣitaṁ
vyatyalaṅkṛtādi-doṣa-tarkitārtha-dūṣitam
dhvasta-yukti-ruddha-buddhi-datta-dhīmadādaraṁ
prema-dhāma-devam eva naumi gaurasundaram

TRANSLATION

The Lord pointed out the defects of ornamental grammar in the verses spontaneously composed and recited in praise of the goddess Gaṅgā by the most celebrated scholar, Keśava Kāśmirī. When the scholar tried to defend himself with many complicated arguments, even those arguments were defeated by the Lord. Although the Lord had humbled the *paṇḍita* by checking his hasty intellect, He nonetheless gave him all due respects and honor as a learned Sanskrit scholar. I sing with joy the unending glories of my golden Gaurasundara, my loving Lord, the one and only abode of divine love.

VERSE 11

सूत्रवृत्तिटिप्पणीष्ठसूक्ष्मवाचनाद्भुतं
धातुमात्रकृष्णशक्तिसर्वविश्वसम्भृतम् ।
रुद्धबुद्धिपण्डितौघनान्ययुक्तिनिर्धरं
प्रेमधामदेवमेव नौमि गौरसुन्दरम् ॥११॥

sūtra-vṛtti-ṭippanīṣṭa-sūkṣma-vācanādbhutaṁ
dhātu-mātra-kṛṣṇa-śakti-sarva-viśva-sambhṛtam
ruddha-buddhi-paṇḍitaugha-nānya-yukti-nirdharaṁ
prema-dhāma-devam eva naumi gaurasundaram

Translation

His wonderful elaborate explanations of the *sūtras* (short but potent Sanskrit aphorisms) were extremely intricate and thereby brought out the natural meanings and diverse aspects. He proved that essentially the *dhātus* (the 7000 root sounds of Sanskrit), in their fullest meaning, express the energies of Kṛṣṇa, the sole supporter of all the universes. The scholarly section were therefore totally perplexed and unable to assert their conclusions before the Lord. They could only sit before Him in dumbfounded astonishment. I sing with joy the unending glories of my beloved Lord, my golden Gaurasundara, the one and only abode of divine love.

Verse 12

कृष्णदृष्टिपातहेतुशब्दकार्थयोजनं
स्फोटवादशृङ्खलैकभित्तिकृष्णवीक्षणम् ।
स्थूलसूक्ष्ममूललक्ष्यकृष्णसौख्यसम्भरं
प्रेमधामदेवमेव नौमि गौरसुन्दरम् ॥१२॥

kṛṣṇa-dṛṣti-pāta-hetu-śabdakārtha-yojanaṁ
sphota-vāda-śṛṅkhalaika-bhitti-kṛṣṇa-vīkṣaṇam
sthūla-sūkṣma-mūla-lakṣya-kṛṣṇa-saukhya-sambharaṁ
prema-dhāma-devam eva naumi gaurasundaram

Translation

He explained that the mutual relationships between all sounds of speech and their meanings (*sphoṭavāda*) have been caused by the single action of Lord Kṛṣṇa's glance. The *sphoṭavāda* scholars weave their grammatical rules and regulations around *sphoṭa*, but factually Kṛṣṇa's sweet will is their only basis. The ultimate purpose of all forms of both subtle and gross energies and their interactions is to provide pleasure to the Supreme Personality of Godhead Śrī Kṛṣna, as an aspect of His transcendental pastimes. I sing with joy the unending glories of my golden Lord Gaurasundara the beautiful, the divine abode of pure love.

VERSE 13

प्रेमरङ्गपाठभङ्गछात्रकाकुकातरं
छात्रसङ्गहस्ततालकीर्त्तनाद्यसञ्चरम् ।
कृष्णनामसीधुसिन्धुमग्नदिक्चराचरं
प्रेमधामदेवमेव नौमि गौरसुन्दरम् ॥१३॥

prema-raṅga-pāṭha-bhaṅga-chātra-kāku-kātaraṁ
chātra-saṅga-hasta-tāla-kīrtanādya-sañcaram
kṛṣṇa-nāma-sīdhu-sindhu-magna-dik-carācaraṁ
prema-dhāma-devam eva naumi gaurasundaram

TRANSLATION

After His return from Gayā it was impossible for the Lord to resume His academic pursuits due to a continuous upsurge of divine love within His heart. His students, forever deprived of that opportunity to study under Nimāi Paṇḍita, condemned themselves as fallen and unfortunate, and with intense imploring humility praised the Lord for His extraordinary genius as a teacher. Although the Lord became very sad due to His compassion for His students, He gave them His blessings and then, being overwhelmed with ecstatic love, began singing *Kṛṣṇa-saṅkīrtana* in the association of those very students. They all joined Him, clapping their hands. This was the auspicious beginning of His *saṅkīrtana* movement. Then all directions became immersed in the sea of nectar that flowed from this ecstatic *kīrtana*. I sing with joy the unending glories of my golden Lord Gaurasundara the beautiful, the divine abode of pure love.

Verse 14

आर्यधर्मपाललब्धदीक्षकृष्णकीर्त्तनं
लक्षलक्षभक्तगीतवाद्यदिव्यनर्त्तनम् ।
धर्मकर्मनाशदस्युदुष्टदुष्कृतोद्धरं
प्रेमधामदेवमेव नौमि गौरसुन्दरम् ॥१४॥

ārya-dharma-pāla-labdha-dīkṣa-kṛṣṇa-kīrtanaṁ
lakṣa-lakṣa-bhakta-gīta-vādya-divya-nartanam
dharma-karma-nāśa-dasyu-duṣṭa-duṣkṛtoddharaṁ
prema-dhāma-devam eva naumi gaurasundaram

Translation

He honors the Vedic religious principles and has taken shelter of His guru's instruction to introduce *Kṛṣṇa-kīrtana*. He is ever absorbed in His ecstatic dance of divine love accompanied by musical instruments amidst the singing and dancing of millions upon millions of devotees. He is the only savior of sinful and evil-minded demons who are responsible for the decline of religion and pious activities in the world. I sing with joy the unending glories of my loving Master Gaurasundara the beautiful, my golden Lord, the divine abode of pure love.

Verse 15

म्लेच्छराजनामबाधभक्तभीतिभञ्जनं
लक्षलक्षदीपनैशकोटिकण्ठकीर्त्तनम् ।

श्रीमृदङ्गतालवाद्यनृत्यकाजिनिस्तरं
प्रेमधामदेवमेव नौमि गौरसुन्दरम् ॥१५॥

mleccha-rāja-nāma-bādha-bhakta-bhīti-bhañjanaṁ
lakṣa-lakṣa-dīpa-naiśa-koṭi-kaṇṭha-kīrtanam
śrī-mṛdaṅga-tāla-vādya-nṛtya-kāji-nistaraṁ
prema-dhāma-devam eva naumi gaurasundaram

TRANSLATION

When the king of *mlecchas* (Chānd Kāzi) obstructed the performance of *hari-nāma*, the Lord removed the fears of His devotees by directing a nocturnal *saṅkīrtana* procession, decorated with hundreds of thousands of lamps and millions of voices singing the Holy Name, dancing to the accompaniment of the sweet sound of the *mṛdaṅga*, *karatālas*, and other musical instruments. He humbled the ruling Kāzi and ultimately won his heart. I sing with joy the unending glories of my loving Gaurasundara, my golden Lord, the divine abode of pure love.

VERSE 16

लक्षलोचनाश्रुवर्षहर्षकेशकर्त्तनं
कोटिकण्ठकृष्णकीर्त्तनाढ्यदण्डधारणम् ।
न्यासिवेशसर्वदेशहाहुताशकातरं
प्रेमधामदेवमेव नौमि गौरसुन्दरम् ॥१६॥

lakṣa-locanāśru-varṣa-harṣa-keśa-kartanaṁ
koṭi-kaṇṭha-kṛṣṇa-kīrtanāḍhya-daṇḍa-dhāraṇam
nyāsi-veśa-sarva-deśa-hā-hutāśa-kātaraṁ
prema-dhāma-devam eva naumi gaurasundaram

Translation

Amidst the showering of tears of sorrow from the eyes of millions, He gladly cut off His beautiful long hair. As He accepted His *daṇḍa*, millions of voices were singing the glories of Kṛṣṇa. Thereafter the people of all lands cried out desperately in grief when they saw Him in the dress of a *sannyāsī*. I sing with joy the unending glories of my golden Lord Gaurasundara the beautiful, the divine abode of pure love.

Verse 17

श्रीयतीशभक्तवेशराढदेशचारणं
कृष्णचैतन्याख्यकृष्णनामजीवतारणम् ।
भावविभ्रमात्ममत्तधावमानभूधरं
प्रेमधामदेवमेव नौमि गौरसुन्दरम् ॥१७॥

śrī-yatīśa-bhakta-veśa-rāḍha-deśa-cāraṇaṁ
kṛṣṇa-caitanyākhya-kṛṣṇa-nāma-jīva-tāraṇam
bhāva-vibhramātma-matta-dhāvamāna-bhūdharaṁ
prema-dhāma-devam eva naumi gaurasundaram

Translation

Being the Lord of all *yogīs*, He wandered over the Rāḍha province (Bengal) as a devotee, thus sanctifying the land with His lotus feet. He was known as Kṛṣṇa Caitanya and rescued all fallen conditioned souls with the Names of Kṛṣṇa. He ran all over the earth just like a madman, intoxicated with transcendental ecstatic loving emotions; His appearance resembled a mountain of gold. I sing with joy the unending glories of my loving Gaurasundara, my golden Lord, the divine abode of pure love.

Verse 18

श्रीगदाधरादिनित्यानन्दसङ्गवर्धनं
अद्वयाख्यभक्तमुख्यवाञ्छितार्थसाधनम् ।
क्षेत्रवाससाभिलाषमात्रतोषतत्परं
प्रेमधाममदेवमेव नौमि गौरसुन्दरम् ॥१८॥

śrī-gadādharādi-nityānanda-saṅga-vardhanaṁ
advayākhya-bhakta-mukhya-vāñchitārtha-sādhanam
kṣetravāsa-sābhilāṣa-mātṛtoṣa-tatparaṁ
prema-dhāma-devam eva naumi gaurasundaram

Translation

His association of devotees became even more prestigious by the presence of exalted personalities like Śrī Gadādhara and Śrī Nityānanda. He descended on earth to fulfill the desires of Advaita Ācārya, the foremost of devotees. To please His mother, He promised that He would not go far away from her but remain close by at Puruṣottama Kṣetra (Jagannātha Purī). I sing with joy the unending glories of my loving Gaurasundara the beautiful, my golden Lord, the divine abode of pure love.

Verse 19

न्यासिराजनीलशैलवाससार्वभौमपं
दाक्षिणात्यतीर्थजातभक्तकल्पपादपम् ।
राममेघरागभक्तिवृष्टिशक्तिसञ्चरं
प्रेमधाममदेवमेव नौमि गौरसुन्दरम् ॥१९॥

nyāsirāja-nīla-śaila-vāsa-sārvabhaumapaṁ
dākṣiṇātya-tīrtha-jāta-bhakta-kalpa-pādapam

rāma-megha-rāga-bhakti-vṛṣṭi-śakti-sañcaraṁ
prema-dhāma-devam eva naumi gaurasundaram

TRANSLATION

When the Lord of *sannyāsīs* reached Nīlācala, He first delivered the famous *paṇḍita* of *Vedānta*, Vāsudeva Sārvabhauma, and then proceeded to southern India where there are many followers of different philosophies. There, like a desire tree, He fulfilled the wishes of the devotees living at various holy places. He met Rāmānanda Rāya who was like a raincloud of devotion, and empowered him to shower everywhere the mellows of spontaneous loving service of Vṛndāvana (*rāga-bhakti*). I sing with joy the unending glories of my loving Gaurasundara, my golden Lord, the divine abode of pure love.

VERSE 20

ध्वस्तसार्वभौमवादनव्यतर्कशङ्करं
ध्वस्ततद्विवर्तवाददानवीयडम्बरम् ।
दर्शितार्थसर्वशास्त्रकृष्णभक्तिमन्दिरं
प्रेमधामदेवमेव नौमि गौरसुन्दरम् ॥२०॥

dhvasta-sārvabhauma-vāda-navya-tarka-śāṅkaraṁ
dhvasta-tadvivarta-vāda-dānavīya-ḍambaram
darśitārtha-sarva-śāstra-kṛṣṇa-bhakti-mandiraṁ
prema-dhāma-devam eva naumi gaurasundaram

TRANSLATION

His original and ever-fresh arguments (delineating the real conclusions of the *Vedas*) devastated the repeated attempts of

Sārvabhauma (by means of *chala, vitaṇḍā, nigraha* and other techniques) to establish *vivartavāda*, the impersonal and atheistic philosophy of Śaṅkara which is supported by proud men with a demoniac and evil mentality. The Lord preached instead that the entire complex of the Vedic scriptures must be viewed as a temple enshrining *Kṛṣṇa-bhakti*. I sing with joy the unending glories of my loving Gaurasundara, my golden Lord, the divine abode of pure love.

Verse 21

प्रेमधामदिव्यदीर्घदेहदेवनन्दितं
हेमकञ्जपुञ्जनिन्दिकान्तिचन्द्रवन्दितम् ।
नामगाननृत्यनव्यदिव्यभावमन्दिरं
प्रेमधामदेवमेव नौमि गौरसुन्दरम् ॥२१॥

prema-dhāma-divya-dīrgha-deha-deva-nanditaṁ
hema-kañja-puñja-nindi-kānti-candra-vanditam
nāma-gāna-nṛtya-navya-divya-bhāva-mandiraṁ
prema-dhāma-devam eva naumi gaurasundaram

Translation

His tall, beautiful, divine figure, the dwelling place of sweet love, greatly increases the pleasure of the demigods. Lovelier than the moon, His effulgent figure mocks the beauty of hundreds of golden lotus flowers. He embodies the ever-fresh moods of transcendental goodness and loving ecstasy arising from the dancing and singing of the Holy Names. I sing with joy the unending glories of my golden Lord Gaurasundara the beautiful, the divine abode of pure love.

VERSE 22

कृष्णकृष्णकृष्णकृष्णकृष्णनामकीर्तनं
रामरामगानरम्यदिव्यचन्दनर्तनम् ।
यत्रतत्रकृष्णनामदानलोकनिस्तरं
प्रेमधामदेवमेव नौमि गौरसुन्दरम् ॥२२॥

kṛṣṇa-kṛṣṇa-kṛṣṇa-kṛṣṇa-kṛṣṇa-nāma-kīrtanaṁ
rāma-rāma-gāna-ramya-divya-chanda-nartanam
yatra-tatra-kṛṣṇa-nāma-dāna-loka-nistaraṁ
prema-dhāma-devam eva naumi gaurasundaram

TRANSLATION

His pilgrimage to South India was actually for the purpose of rescuing the residents of that place. At roadsides, temples and holy sanctuaries He would chant in sweet tunes "Kṛṣṇa Kṛṣṇa Kṛṣṇa Kṛṣṇa Kṛṣṇa Kṛṣṇa Kṛṣṇa hey!" Sometimes carried away by some indescribable divine exultation, He would sing "Rāma Rāma" and dance sweetly in ecstatic rhythm. He would deliver one and all, irrespective of time, place or circumstance, by magnanimously inducing them to chant the Holy Names of Kṛṣṇa. I sing with joy the unending glories of my golden Lord Gaurasundara, the divine abode of pure love.

VERSE 23

गोदावर्यावामतीररामानन्दसंवादं
ज्ञानकर्ममुक्तमर्मरागभक्तिसंपदम् ।
पारकीयकान्तकृष्णभावसेवनाकरं
प्रेमधामदेवमेव नौमि गौरसुन्दरम् ॥२३॥

godāvarya-vāma-tīra-rāmānanda-saṁvadaṁ
jñāna-karma-mukta-marma-rāga-bhakti-sampadam
pārakīya-kānta-kṛṣṇa-bhāva-sevanākaraṁ
prema-dhāma-devam eva naumi gaurasundaram

TRANSLATION

In His famous conversation with Rāmānanda Rāya which is known as *Rāmānanda Saṁvāda* in *Śrī Caitanya-caritāmṛta*, He concluded that the most cherished possession is *rāga-bhakti*, or spontaneous loving service to the Lord, rendered with a heart which has been thoroughly cleansed of *jñāna* (knowledge) and *karma* (fruitive activities), and that Kṛṣṇa, the Master of *pārakīya* conjugal love, is the only basis, the singular objective and the sole recipient of *bhāva-sevā* or ecstatic loving service. I sing with joy the unending glories of my golden Lord Gaurasundara the beautiful, the divine abode of pure love.

VERSE 24

दास्यसख्यवात्स्यकान्तसेवनोत्तरोत्तरं
श्रेष्ठपारकीयराधिकाङ्घ्रिभक्तिसुन्दरम् ।
श्रीव्रजस्वसिद्धदिव्यकामकृष्णतत्परं
प्रेमधामदेवमेव नौमि गौरसुन्दरम् ॥२४॥

dāsya-sakhya-vātsya-kānta-sevanottarottaraṁ
śreṣṭha-pārakīya-rādhikāṅghri-bhakti-sundaram
śrī-vraja-svasiddha-divya-kāma-kṛṣṇa-tatparaṁ
prema-dhāma-devam eva naumi gaurasundaram

TRANSLATION

He showed that one may serve the Lord in variegated devotional relationships progressing in excellence from servitude to friendship, to parenthood and conjugal love, and ultimately that pure devotional service to the lotus feet of Śrīmatī Rādhārāṇī in moods of sweet *pārakīya* conjugal love for Vrajendra-nandana is the most beautiful. Divine and spontaneous loving desires in the most pure and pristine form can have their full meaning only in Śrī Vrajendra-nandana, Śrī Kṛṣṇa in Vraja Dhāma—such realization was given by Śrīman Mahāprabhu. I sing with joy the unending glories of my golden Lord Gaurasundara the beautiful, the divine abode of pure love.

VERSE 25

शान्तमुक्तभृत्यतृप्तमित्रमत्तदर्शितं
स्निग्धमुग्धशिष्टमिष्टसुष्टकुण्ठहर्षितम् ।
तन्त्रमुक्तवाम्यरागसर्वसेवनोत्तरं
प्रेमधामदेवमेव नौमि गौरसुन्दरम् ॥२५॥

śānta-mukta-bhṛtya-tṛpta-mitra-matta-darśitaṁ
snigdha-mugdha-śiṣṭa-miṣṭa-suṣṭha-kuṇṭha-harśitam
tantra-mukta-vāmya-rāga-sarva-sevanottaraṁ
prema-dhāma-devam eva naumi gaurasundaram

TRANSLATION

He explained that the devotee in the mood of passive adoration enjoys the pleasure of liberation from suffering, and the devotee in the service mood enjoys the pleasure of contentment in service. The devotee in friendship enjoys the pleasure of serving the Lord directly under His shelter, while the devotee in parental relationship simply enjoys intense affection for the Lord as a son. He further revealed that the devotee in *svakīya* conjugal love is restricted in enjoying the sweet nectars and full nourishment of *mādhurya*, due to the impositions of scriptural injunctions. However, when the service in *mādhurya* becomes free of the bindings of scriptural regulations and is full of *pārakīya* conjugal loving moods of Vraja, especially when the element *vāmya* is added—such service gives Kṛṣṇa the greatest pleasure. I sing with joy the unending glories of my golden Lord Gaurasundara the beautiful, the divine abode of pure love.

Verse 26

आत्मनव्यतत्त्वदिव्यरायभाग्यदर्शितं
श्यामगोपराधिकाप्तकोक्तगुप्तचेष्टितम् ।
मूर्च्छिताङ्घ्रिरामरायबोधितात्मकिङ्करं
प्रेमधाममदेवमेव नौमि गौरसुन्दरम् ॥२६॥

ātma-navya-tattva-divya-rāya-bhāgya-darśitaṁ
śyāma-gopa-rādhikāpta-kokta-gupta-ceṣṭitam
murcchitāṅghri-rāmarāya-bodhitātma-kiṅkaraṁ
prema-dhāma-devam eva naumi gaurasundaram

Translation

He revealed to the fortunate Śrī Rāya how He had personally descended to perform His ever-fresh divine pastimes at Navadvīpa. When Rāmānanda thus beheld before his eyes the Lord's own form as the cowherd boy Śyāmasundara, appearing with the nature of mysterious love in the mood and luster of Śrī Rādhikā, he fell down unconscious before the lotus feet of the Lord. The kind Lord then Himself restored the consciousness of His eternally surrendered servant. I sing with joy the unending glories of my golden Lord Gaurasundara the beautiful, the divine abode of pure love.

Verse 27

नष्टकुष्ठकूर्मविप्ररूपभक्तितोषणं
रामदासविप्रमोहमुक्तभक्तपोषणम् ।
कालकृष्णदासमुक्तभट्टथारिपिञ्जरं
प्रेमधामदेवमेव नौमि गौरसुन्दरम् ॥२७॥

naṣṭa-kuṣṭha-kūrma-vipra-rūpa-bhakti-toṣaṇaṁ
rāmadāsa-vipra-moha-mukta-bhakta-poṣaṇam
kāla-kṛṣṇa-dāsa-mukta-bhaṭṭathāri-piñjaraṁ
prema-dhāma devam eva naumi gaurasundaram

Translation

At Kūrma-kṣetra, near Jagannātha Purī, He pleased the *brāhmaṇa* devotee by warmly embracing him and thereby cured his leprosy and awarded him a beautiful body. By quoting the *Kūrma Purāṇa*, He dispelled all the fear and illusion of the South Indian *brāhmaṇa* who was under the misimpression that his worshipable Goddess Sītā was touched by a demon. He showed that the transcendental is beyond all material contamination, and endowed him with pure devotion. He saved the ignorant *brāhmaṇa* Kālakṛṣṇa, who had been lured by *māyā* into the hands of the infamous Bhaṭṭathāri sect of Mālāvara. All glories, all glories to my golden Lord Gaurasundara the beautiful, the divine abode of pure love.

Verse 28

रङ्गनाथभट्टभक्तितुष्टभङ्गिभाषणं
लक्ष्म्यगम्यकृष्णरासगोपिकैकपोषणम् ।
लक्ष्म्यभीष्टकृष्णशीर्षसाध्यसाधनाकरं
प्रेमधामदेवमेव नौमि गौरसुन्दरम् ॥२८॥

raṅganātha-bhaṭṭa-bhakti-tuṣṭa-bhaṅgi-bhāṣaṇaṁ
lakṣmyagamya-kṛṣṇa-rāsa-gopikaika-poṣaṇam
lakṣmyabhīṣṭa-kṛṣṇa-śīrṣa-sādhya-sādhanākaraṁ
prema-dhāma-devam eva naumi gaurasundaram

TRANSLATION

Being pleased with the service of Vyeṅkaṭa Bhaṭṭa at Raṅga-kṣetra (situated on the banks of the Kāverī) where the Vaiṣṇavas firmly believe that worship of Lakṣmī-Nārāyaṇa is the ultimate objective, the Lord, in a seemingly playful mood, instructed him that the *rāsa* pastimes of Kṛṣṇa are fully maintained, supported, and protected by the *gopīs*. Since Kṛṣṇa is ultimately the superexcellent goal of all desirable objects, even Lakṣmī Devī is attracted by Him. I sing with joy the unending glories of my golden Lord, Gaurasundara the beautiful, the divine abode of pure love.

VERSE 29

ब्रह्मसंहिताख्यकृष्णभक्तिशास्त्रदायकं
कृष्णकर्णसीधुनामकृष्णकाव्यगायकम् ।
श्रीप्रतापरुद्रराजशीर्षसेव्यमन्दिरं
प्रेमधामदेवमेव नौमि गौरसुन्दरम् ॥२९॥

brahma-saṁhitākhya-kṛṣṇa-bhakti-śāstra-dāyakaṁ
kṛṣṇa-karṇa-sīdhu-nāma-kṛṣṇa-kāvya-gāyakam
śrī-pratāparudra-rāja-śīrṣa-sevya-mandiraṁ
prema-dhāma-devam eva naumi gaurasundaram

TRANSLATION

He gave His devotee *Brahma-saṁhitā*, the famous scripture

which is full of the conclusions of devotion to Lord Kṛṣṇa. He lovingly sang the lyrical verses which depict *Vraja-līlā* from the book *Kṛṣṇa-karṇāmṛtam* composed by the South Indian poet Bilvamaṅgala Ṭhākura. King Pratāparudra worshiped His lotus feet by bowing down and placing them on his head. I sing with joy the unending glories of my golden Lord Gaurasundara the beautiful, the divine abode of pure love.

Verse 30

श्रीरथाग्रभक्तगीतदिव्यनर्त्तनाद्भुतं
यात्रिपात्रमित्ररुद्रराजहृच्चमत्कृतम् ।
गुण्डिचागमादितत्त्वरूपकाव्यसञ्चरं
प्रेमधामदेवमेव नौमि गौरसुन्दरम् ॥३०॥

śrī-rathāgra-bhakta-gīta-divya-nartanādbhutaṁ
yātri-pātra-mitra-rudrarāja-hṛccamatkṛtam
guṇḍicāgamādi-tattva-rūpa-kāvya-sañcaraṁ
prema-dhāma-devam eva naumi gaurasundaram

Translation

Surrounded by devotees absorbed in *saṅkīrtana* in front of the chariot, He appeared as the divine and wonderful Naṭarāja, the King of dancers, astounding the journeying pilgrims and the friends and relatives of King Pratāparudra, thus filling their hearts with wonder. By His potency, the natural purport of the pastime of Lord Jagannātha's chariot ride to Guṇḍicā was manifested in the poem composed by Śrīla Rūpa Gosvāmī (*priyaḥ so'yaṁ...vipināya spṛhayati*). All glories, all glories to my golden Lord Gaurasundara the beautiful, the divine abode of pure love.

Verse 31

प्रेममुग्धरुद्रराजशौर्यवीर्यविक्रमं
प्रार्थितङ्घ्रिवर्जितान्यसर्वधर्मसङ्गमम् ।
लुण्ठितप्रतापशीर्षपादधूलिधूसरं
प्रेमधामदेवमेव नौमि गौरसुन्दरम् ॥३१॥

prema-mugdha-rudra-rāja-śaurya-vīrya-vikramaṁ
prārthitāṅghri-varjitānya-sarva-dharma-saṅgamam
luṇṭhita-pratāpa-śīrṣa-pāda-dhuli-dhūsaraṁ
prema-dhāma-devam eva naumi gaurasundaram

Translation

Wonderstruck and overwhelmed by the Lord's genius, effulgence and loving symptoms, King Pratāparudra of Utkala gave up all previous religious conceptions and traditions, along with all sense of royal glory, heroism, and power. Then, with a single-minded craving for the Lord, the king threw himself before His lotus feet to be crowned with their dust. I sing with joy the unending glories of my golden Lord, Gaurasundara the beautiful, the divine abode of pure love.

Verse 32

दाक्षिणात्यसुप्रसिद्धपण्डितौघपूजितं
श्रेष्ठराजराजपात्रशीर्षभक्तिभूषितम् ।
देशमातृशेषदर्शनार्थिगौडगोचरं
प्रेमधामदेवमेव नौमि गौरसुन्दरम् ॥३२॥

dākṣiṇātya-suprasiddha-paṇḍitaugha-pūjitaṁ
śreṣṭha-rāja-rājapātra-śirṣa-bhakti-bhūṣitam

deśa-mātṛ-śeṣa-darśanārthi-gauṛa-gocaraṁ
prema-dhāma-devam eva naumi gaurasundaram

TRANSLATION

When the Lord was in South India, the famous scholars there worshiped Him, and powerful kings, their ministers and family members honored and revered Him—He was their crown jewel of devotion. Then, according to the custom of *sannyāsīs*, He turned homeward towards Bengal, to see His mother, motherland, and the Gaṅgā for the last time. I sing with joy the unending glories of my golden Lord, Gaurasundara the beautiful, the divine abode of pure love.

VERSE 33

गौरगर्विसर्वगौडगौरवार्थसज्जितं
शास्त्रशस्त्रदक्षदुष्टनास्तिकादिलज्जितम् ।
मुह्यमानमातृकादिदेहजीवसञ्चरं
प्रेमधामदेवमेव नौमि गौरसुन्दरम् ॥३३॥

gaura-garvi-sarva-gauḍa-gauravārtha-sajjitaṁ
śāstra-śastra-dakṣa-duṣṭa-nāstikādi-lajjitam
muhyamāna-mātṛkādi-deha-jīva-sañcaraṁ
prema-dhāma-devam eva naumi gaurasundaram

TRANSLATION

As the fame of the Lord spread far and wide and news came of His arrival, all of Bengal, proud of their Lord, prepared to receive and glorify Him. Even the handful of puffed-up atheists and skeptics were ashamed of their lowliness when they saw how the multitudes honored and loved the Lord. Upon His arrival, He revitalized and rejuvenated His mother and other devotees who were dying due to separation from Him. I sing with joy the unending glories of my golden Lord Gaurasundara the beautiful, the divine abode of pure love.

VERSE 34

न्यासपञ्चवर्षपूर्णजन्मभूमिदर्शनं
कोटिकोटिलोकलुब्धमुग्धदृष्टिकर्षणम् ।
कोटिकण्ठकृष्णनामघोषभेदिताम्बरं
प्रेमधामदेवमेव नौमि गौरसुन्दरम् ॥३४॥

nyāsa-pañca-varṣa-pūrṇa-janma-bhūmi-darśanaṁ
koṭi-koṭi-loka-lubdha-mugdha-dṛṣṭi-karṣaṇam
koṭi-kaṇṭha-kṛṣṇa-nāma-ghoṣa-bheditāmvaraṁ
prema-dhāma-devam eva naumi gaurasundaram

TRANSLATION

When at last he returned to his motherland, Bengal, after five long years of *sannyāsa*, millions of people rushed to see Him. Deeply moved, with eyes full of eagerness, they beheld their Lord who attracts the hearts of everyone. There was a tumultuous and continuous uproar that spread in all directions and pierced the skies, as millions upon millions of voices repeatedly resounded the Holy Names of Hari. I sing with joy the unending glories of my golden Lord Gaurasundara the beautiful, the divine abode of pure love.

VERSE 35

आर्तभक्तशोकशान्तितापिपापिपावनं
लक्षकोटिलोकसङ्गकृष्णधामधावनम् ।

रामकेलिसाग्रजातरूपकर्षणादरं
प्रेमधामदेवमेव नौमि गौरसुन्दरम् ॥३५॥

ārta-bhakta-śoka-śānti-tāpi-pāpi-pāvanaṁ
lakṣa-koṭi-loka-saṅga-kṛṣṇa-dhāma-dhāvanam
rāma-keli-sāgrajāta-rūpa-karṣaṇādaraṁ
prema-dhāma-devam eva naumi gaurasundaram

TRANSLATION

After having pacified His devotees who were heartbroken due to not being able to see their Master for such a long time, and after having delivered and pardoned many sinners and miserable persons (such as Cāpāla Gopāla, etc.), He began to run towards Vṛndāvana, the abode of Kṛṣṇa, with thousands of millions of people in His wake. On the way, at Rāmakeli, He was attracted by Śrī Rūpa and his elder brother Śrī Sanātana to whom He expressed feelings of love. I sing with joy the unending glories of my golden Lord, Gaurasundara the beautiful, the divine abode of pure love.

VERSE 36

व्याघ्रवारणैनवन्यजन्तुकृष्णगायकं
प्रेमनृत्यभावमत्तझाडखण्डनायकम् ।
दुर्गवन्यमार्गभट्टमात्रसङ्गसौकरं
प्रेमधामदेवमेव नौमि गौरसुन्दरम् ॥३६॥

vyāghra-vāraṇaina-vanya-jantu-kṛṣṇa-gāyakaṁ
prema-nṛtya-bhāva-matta-jhāḍakhaṇḍa-nāyakam
durga-vanya-mārga-bhaṭṭa-mātra-saṅga-saukaraṁ
prema-dhāma-devam eva naumi gaurasundaram

TRANSLATION

As He went on, the Lord came upon Jhāḍikhaṇḍa forest where He magically induced tigers, deer, elephants and other forest creatures to sing with Him the Names of Kṛṣṇa. Dancing sweetly in the mood of divine love and maddened by ecstasy, the Lord easily proceeded through inaccessible forest paths, accompanied only by Balabhadra Bhaṭṭācārya. I sing with joy the unending glories of my golden Lord, Gaurasundara the beautiful, the divine abode of pure love.

VERSE 37

गाङ्गयामुनादिबिन्दुमाधवादिमाननं
माथुरार्त्तचित्तयामुनाग्रभागधावनम् ।
स्मारितव्रजातितीव्रविप्रलम्भकातरं
प्रेमधामदेवमेव नौमि गौरसुन्दरम् ॥३७॥

gāṅga-yāmunādi-bindu-mādhavādi-mānanaṁ
māthurārta-citta-yāmunāgra-bhāga-dhāvanam
smārita-vrajāti-tīvra-vipralambha-kātaraṁ
prema-dhāma-devam eva naumi gaurasundaram

TRANSLATION

At Prayāga and Vārāṇasī, on the banks of the Gaṅgā and Yamunā rivers, He visited many temples and offered His respects to the Bindu-Mādhava Deity and the other Deities there. Then, anxious to visit Mathurā, He began to run along the bank of the Yamunā towards the city, following the current of the river. As thoughts of *Vraja-līlā* arose in His mind, He became fully merged in intense separation from Vraja. I sing with joy the unending glories of my golden Lord Gaurasundara the beautiful, the divine abode of pure love.

VERSE 38

माधवेन्द्रविप्रलम्भमाथुरेष्टमाननं
प्रेमधामदृष्टकामपूर्वकुञ्जकाननम् ।
गोकुलादिगोष्ठगोपगोपिकाप्रियङ्करं
प्रेमधामदेवमेव नौमि गौरसुन्दरम् ॥३८॥

mādhavendra-vipralambha-māthureṣṭa-mānanaṁ
prema-dhāma-dṛṣṭa-kāma-pūrva-kuñja-kānanam
gokulādi-goṣṭha-gopa-gopikā-priyaṅkaraṁ
prema-dhāma-devam eva naumi gaurasundaram

TRANSLATION

He relished the mood of separation (*vipralambha*) tasted by Mādhavendra Purī in his compositions describing Śrī Rādhikā's lamenations ("*ayi dīnadayārdra-nātha…kiṁ karomyaham*", "*mathurā mathurā…madhurā madhurā*" etc.) for Her beloved Kṛṣṇa who had left for Mathurā. He finally beheld before His eyes Vṛndāvana, the divine abode of love, and absorbed to His heart's content the scenes of beautiful flower gardens and forests where He had previously performed His pastimes. He displayed affectionate dealings with the *gopas* and *gopīs* in the twelve forests of Vṛndāvana (Gokula and others). I sing with joy the unending glories of my golden Gaurasundara the beautiful, the divine abode of pure love.

VERSE 39

प्रेमगुञ्जनालिपुञ्जपुष्पपुञ्जरञ्जितं
गीतनृत्यदक्षपक्षिवृक्षलक्षवन्दितम् ।

गोवृषादिनाददीप्तपूर्वमोदमेदुरं
प्रेमधामदेवमेव नौमि गौरसुन्दरम् ॥३९॥

prema-guñjanāli-puñja-puṣpa-puñja-rañjitaṁ
gīta-nṛtya-dakṣa-pakṣi-vṛkṣa-lakṣa-vanditam
go-vṛṣādi-nāda-dīpta-pūrva-moda-meduraṁ
prema-dhāma-devam eva naumi gaurasundaram

Translation

As He walked through the groves of Vṛndāvana, beautiful flowers surrounded by bumblebees humming in sweet drones would lovingly glorify Him wherever He went. Birds adept at singing and dancing would honor Him with their song, and thousands of trees would offer Him their obeisances. At once the memory would be aroused of how the cows, calves, and oxen would lovingly call out to Him, and His heart would be overflooded with love. In this way the Lord would relive His previous pastimes in ecstasy. I sing with joy the unending glories of my golden Lord Gaurasundara the beautiful, the divine abode of pure love.

Verse 40

प्रेमबुद्धरुद्धबुद्धिमत्तनृत्यकीर्त्तनं
प्लाविताश्रुकाञ्चनाङ्गवासचातुरङ्गनम् ।
कृष्णकृष्णरावभावहास्यलास्यभास्वरं
प्रेमधामदेवमेव नौमि गौरसुन्दरम् ॥४०॥

prema-buddha-ruddha-buddhi-matta-nṛtya-kīrtanaṁ
plāvitāśru-kāñcanāṅga-vāsa-cāturaṅganam
kṛṣṇa-kṛṣṇa-rāva-bhāva-hāsya-lāsya-bhāsvaraṁ
prema-dhāma-devam eva naumi gaurasundaram

TRANSLATION

Totally absorbed in divine love, He would lose all sensation of the external world, and sing the Holy Names and dance, just like a madman. The tears that flowed incessantly from His eyes drenched His form of molten gold and His bright garments, and would flood the ground in all directions. In the mood of *mahā-bhāva* He would break out in loud laughter and irresistibly cry at the top of his voice, "Kṛṣṇa! Kṛṣṇa!" In this way, by His many different postures, the brilliance of His beauty was exhibited more and more. I sing with joy the unending glories of my golden Lord Gaurasundara the beautiful, the divine abode of pure love.

VERSE 41

प्रेममुग्धनृत्यकीर्त्तनाकुलारिटान्तिकं
स्नानधन्यवारिधान्यभूमिकुण्डदेशकम् ।
प्रेमकुण्डराधिकाख्यशास्त्रवन्दनादरं
प्रेमधामदेवमेव नौमि गौरसुन्दरम् ॥४१॥

prema-mugdha-nṛtya-kīrtanākulāriṭāntikaṁ
snāna-dhanya-vāri-dhānya-bhūmi-kuṇḍa-deśakam
prema-kuṇḍa-rādhikākhya-śāstra-vandanādaraṁ
prema-dhāma-devam eva naumi gaura-sundaram

TRANSLATION

Thus enraptured in divine love, the Lord, dancing and singing the glories of Kṛṣṇa, approached the sacred pond, Śrī Rādhā-kuṇḍa. He blessed the water of the paddy fields by bathing in it, thereby revealing that very spot to be Rādhā-kuṇḍa. He then imploringly sang verses from the scriptures worshiping and glorifying that divine lake of love, named after the Supreme

Consort Śrīmatī Rādhārāṇī. I sing with joy the unending glories of my golden Lord Gaurasundara the beautiful, the divine abode of pure love.

Verse 42

तिन्तिडीतलस्थयामुनोर्मिभावनाप्लुतं
निर्जनैकराधिकात्मभाववैभवावृतम् ।
श्यामराधिकाप्तगौरतत्त्वभित्तिकाकरं
प्रेमधामदेवमेव नौमि गौरसुन्दरम् ॥४२॥

tintiḍī-talastha-yāmunormi-bhāvanāplutaṁ
nirjanaika-rādhikātma-bhāva-vaibhavāvṛtam
śyāma-rādhikāpta-gaura-tattva-bhittikākaraṁ
prema-dhāma-devam eva naumi gaurasundaram

Translation

While He was visiting the various places of pastimes in Vṛndāvana, the Lord arrived at the famous tamarind tree (which had been existing since the Dvāpara-yuga). He sat beneath its branches, and when He saw the dancing waves of Yamunā, the memory of *jala-keli* was aroused within Him, and He became immersed in thoughts of those confidential sporting pastimes of Lord Kṛṣṇa with the *gopīs* in the water. In that secluded place, undisturbed, His whole being became pervaded with thoughts of Rādhikā, Her beauty and Her sweetness. This place is indicated to be the place of origin of *Gaura-tattva*, for it was here that Śyāmasundara was totally absorbed in ecstatic love for Śrīmatī Rādhārāṇī. Śrīman Mahāprabhu, who is Himself the origin of all, eternally resides in this place. I sing with joy the unending glories of my golden Lord Gaurasundara the beautiful, the divine abode of pure love.

VERSE 43

शारिकाशुकोक्तिकौतुकाढ्यलास्यलापितं
राधिकाव्यतीतकामदेवकाममोहितम् ।
प्रेमवश्यकृष्णभावभक्तहृच्चमत्कृतं
प्रेमधामदेवमेव नौमि गौरसुन्दरम् ॥४३॥

sārikā-śukokti-kautukāḍhya-lāsya-lāpitaṁ
rādhikā-vyatīta-kāmadeva-kāma-mohitam
prema-vaśya-kṛṣṇa-bhāva-bhakta-hṛccamatkaraṁ
prema-dhāma-devam eva naumi gaurasundaram

TRANSLATION

He was the subject of the witty and humorous conversation between the parrot and his mate in which the supreme cupid, Śrī Kṛṣṇa, is described as bewildered by longing desire in the absence of Śrī Rādhikā. Through this dialogue the Lord filled the devotees' hearts with wonder by revealing that the sweetness of Kṛṣṇa's character is that He can be subdued by love. I sing with joy the unending glories of my golden Lord Gaurasundara the beautiful, the divine abode of pure love.

VERSE 44

श्रीप्रयागधामरूपरागभक्तिसञ्चरं
श्रीसनातनादिकाशिभक्तिशिक्षणादरम् ।
वैष्णवानुरोधभेदनिर्विशेषपञ्जरं
प्रेमधामदेवमेव नौमि गौरसुन्दरम् ॥४४॥

śrī-prayāga-dhāma-rūpa-rāga-bhakti-sañcaraṁ
śrī-sanātanādi-kāśi-bhakti-śikṣaṇādaram
vaiṣṇavānurodha-bheda-nirviśeṣa-pañjaraṁ
prema-dhāma-devam eva naumi gaurasundaram

TRANSLATION

At Prayāga Dhāma, the Lord empowered Śrīla Rūpa Gosvāmī to understand and expound the means and end of divine love in the mood of Vṛndāvana. At Kāśī Dhāma He affectionately taught Śrīla Sanātana Gosvāmī and others the principles and practices of pure devotion. At the request of the Vaiṣṇavas present, He destroyed the stubborn pride of the narrow-minded impersonalists of Kāśī, who blindly believed in self-worship, thus giving them the freedom of devotion unto Parabrahma, the Supreme Absolute Truth. I sing with joy the unending glories of my golden Lord Gaurasundara the beautiful, the divine abode of pure love.

VERSE 45

न्यासिलक्षनायकप्रकाशानन्दतारकं
न्यासिराशिकाशिवासिकृष्णनामपारकम् ।
व्यासनारदादिदत्तवेदधीधुरन्धरं
प्रेमधामदेवमेव नौमि गौरसुन्दरम् ॥४५॥

nyāsi-lakṣa-nāyaka-prakāśānanda-tārakaṁ
nyāsi-rāśi-kāśi-vāsi-kṛṣṇa-nāma-pārakam
vyāsa-nāradādi-datta-vedadhī-dhurandharaṁ
prema-dhāma-devam eva nuami gaura-sundaram

TRANSLATION

After Prakāśānanda Sarasvatī, the leader of hundreds of thousands of Māyāvādī *sannyāsīs*, was rescued from the pit of impersonalism by the Lord, He delivered the residents of Kāśī, who were primarily *sannyāsīs*, from the ocean of birth and death by bestowing the Holy Names of Lord Kṛṣṇa upon them. The Lord is the transcendental support of the chariot of the nectarean conclusions of the Vedic scriptures which are handed down in disciplic succession coming through Nārada and Vyāsa. I sing with joy the unending glories of my golden Gaurasundara the beautiful, the divine abode of pure love.

VERSE 46

ब्रह्मसूत्रभाष्यकृष्णनारदोपदेशकं
श्लोकतुर्यभाषणान्तकृष्णसंप्रकाशकम् ।
शब्दवर्त्तनान्तहेतुनामजीवनिस्तरं
प्रेमधामदेवमेव नौमि गौरसुन्दरम् ॥४६॥

brahma-sūtra-bhāṣya-kṛṣṇa-nāradopadeśakaṁ
śloka-tūrya-bhāṣaṇānta-kṛṣṇa-samprakāśakam
śabda-vartanānta-hetu-nāma-jīva-nistaraṁ
prema-dhāma-devam eva naumi gaura-sundaram

TRANSLATION

At Kāśī, in the assembly of Māyāvādī *sannyāsīs*, He taught that *Śrīmad Bhāgavatam* is the natural commentary on the *Brahma-sūtra*, exactly as passed down from Śrī Kṛṣṇa to Brahmā to Nārada in the *paramparā* disciplic succession. After His explanation of the *catuḥ-ślokī* (four root verses of the *Bhāgavatam*), He brilliantly revealed the non-dual Supreme Absolute Truth, the self-effulgent source of the cosmos, the Supreme Personality of Godhead Śrī Kṛṣṇa. He ascertained that only *śabda-brahma*, or the transcendental sound vibration of the Holy Names of Kṛṣṇa, awards the highest auspiciousness of releasing the living entities from the cycle of birth and death. I sing with joy the unending glories of my golden Lord Gaurasundara the beautiful, the divine abode of pure love.

VERSE 47

आत्मरामवाचनादिनिर्विशेषखण्डनं
श्रौतवाक्यसार्थकैकचिद्विलासमण्डनम् ।
दिव्यकृष्णविग्रहादिगौणबुद्धिधिक्करं
प्रेमधामदेवमेव नौमि गौरसुन्दरम् ॥४७॥

ātma-rāma-vācanādi-nirviśeṣa-khaṇḍanaṁ
śrauta-vākya-sārthakaika-cidvilāsa-maṇḍanam
divya-kṛṣṇa-vigrahādi-gauṇa-buddhi-dhikkaraṁ
prema-dhāma-devam eva naumi gaurasundaram

TRANSLATION

He cut to pieces the impersonalist doctrines of Śaṅkarācārya, by His exposition of sixty-one different explanations of the famous *ātmarāma* verse of *Śrīmad Bhāgavatam*. With the help of numerous scriptural references, He brought to light the Supreme Lord`s sweet transcendental pastimes. He strongly denounced the hateful conception that the worshipable Deity forms of Kṛṣṇa are a mere transformation of the illusory material modes of goodness. I sing with joy the unending glories of my golden Lord Gaurasundara the beautiful, the divine abode of pure love.

VERSE 48

ब्रह्मपारमात्म्यलक्षणाद्वयैकवाचनं
श्रीव्रजस्वसिद्धनन्दलीलनन्दनन्दनम् ।

श्रीरसस्वरूपरासलीलगोपसुन्दरं
प्रेमधामदेवमेव नौमि गौरसुन्दरम् ॥४८॥

brahma-pāramātmya-lakṣaṇādvayaika-vācanaṁ
śrī-vraja-svasiddha-nanda-līla-nanda-nandanam
śrī-rasa-svarūpa-rāsa-līla-gopa-sundaraṁ
prema-dhāma-devam eva naumi gaurasundaram

TRANSLATION

By citing the *Śrīmad Bhāgavatam* verse (*brahmeti paramātmeti bhagavān iti śabdyate*) and thus accomodating both the conceptions of *brahman* and *paramātmā* which are considered by the *jñānīs* and *yogīs* respectively to be their ultimate goals, the Lord showed how *brahman* and *paramātmā* are included within and surpassed by the highest conception, *bhagavān*, who is the sum and substance of knowledge of the Absolute Truth, the supreme primeval principle of all spiritual relationships, the Supreme Personality of Godhead Himself.

Then, by introducing the self-evident, confidential and blissful pastimes, the Lord indicated that certainly above Vaikuṇṭha (*vaikuṇṭhāj janito varā madhupūrī*) in the supreme and inconceivable eternal abode of Vṛndāvana, the Absolute Truth, the Supreme Personality of Godhead Nanda-nandana appears, fulfilling the aim of His divine sonhood.

And ultimately, considering the fullest conception of *rasa-tattva* in full-fledged theism, Śrīman Mahāprabhu then revealed the real nature of the complete embodiment of divine ecstasies through his acceptance of consorthood in the original and principal *rasa* (*madhurya-rasa*), the aggregate of all *rasas*. At the same time, He indicated that the divine playful amorous pastimes of *rāsa-līlā* conducted by the personal potency of the all-beautiful is exclusively the highest goal of the living entities. I sing with joy the unending glories of my golden

Lord Gaurasundara the beautiful, the divine abode of pure love.

VERSE 49

राधिकाविनोदमात्रतत्त्वलक्षणान्वयं
साधुसङ्गकृष्णनामसाधनैकनिश्चयम् ।
प्रेमसेवनैकमात्रसाध्यकृष्णतत्परं
प्रेमधामदेवमेव नौमि गौरसुन्दरम् ॥४९॥

rādhikā-vinoda-mātra-tattva-lakṣaṇānvayaṁ
sādhu-saṅga-kṛṣṇa-nāma-sādhanaika-niścayam
prema-sevanaika-mātra-sādhya-kṛṣṇa-tatparaṁ
prema-dhāma-devam eva naumi gaurasundaram

TRANSLATION

In an assembly of intellectuals, He (the Supreme Lord, always absorbed in perfectional loving pastimes with Śrīmatī Rādhārāṇī) determined Rādhā-Vinoda to be the sole *sambandha-tattva* or exclusive essence of all knowledge of spiritual relationships, which descends by disciplic succession. He also determined the chanting of the Holy Names of Kṛṣṇa in the association of saints to be the definite method (*abhidheya*) of attaining the highest achievable goal (*prayojana*) which is loving devotional service unto Gopījana-vallabha, Kṛṣṇa, the beloved of Śrī Rādhikā. I sing with joy the unending glories of my golden Lord Gaurasundara the beautiful, the divine abode of pure love.

VERSE 50

आत्मारामवाचनैकषष्टिकार्थदर्शितं
रुद्रसंख्यशब्दजातयद्यदर्थसंभृतम् ।

सर्वसर्वयुक्ततत्तदर्थभूरिदाकरं
प्रेमधामदेवमेव नौमि गौरसुन्दरम् ॥५०॥

ātma-rāma-vācanaika-ṣaṣṭikārtha-darśitaṁ
rudra-saṁkhya-śabda-jāta-yadyadartha-sambhṛtam
sarva-sarva-yukta-ıattadartha-bhūridākaraṁ
prema-dhāma-devam eva naumi gaurasundaram

Translation

He gave sixty-one different explanations of the *ātmārāma* verse of the *Śrīmad Bhāgavatam*. By separately combining, one after another, the several intrinsic meanings of each of the eleven words of this verse, He showed the *śloka* to be a treasure-house full of purports in line with the *śuddha-bhakti-siddhānta* or the conclusions of pure devotion. I sing with joy the unending glories of my golden Lord Gaurasundara the beautiful, the divine abode of pure love.

Verse 51

श्रीसनातनानुरूपजीवसम्प्रदायकं
लुप्ततीर्थशुद्धभक्तिशास्त्रसुप्रचारकम् ।
नीलशैलनाथपीठनैजकार्यसौकरं
प्रेमधामदेवमेव नौमि गौरसुन्दरम् ॥५१॥

śrī-sanātanānu-rūpa-jīva-sampradāyakaṁ
lupta-tīrtha-śuddha-bhakti-śāstra-supracārakam
nīla-śaila-nātha-pīṭha-naija-kārya-saukaraṁ
prema-dhāma-devam eva naumi gaurasundaram

Translation

He established and revealed His *sampradāya* through Śrī

Sanātana, his younger brother Śrī Rūpa, Śrī Jīva, and their followers. He unveiled the location of many holy places and perfectly preached the *śuddha-bhakti śāstras* or scriptures of pure devotion. He lovingly revealed the true concept of worship to Himself before the servitors of Śrī Jagannātha Deva at Nīlācala. I sing with joy the unending glories of my golden Gaurasundara the beautiful, the divine abode of pure love.

VERSE 52

त्यागवाह्यभोगबुद्धितीव्रदण्डनिन्दनं
रायशुद्धकृष्णकामसेवनाभिनन्दनम् ।
रायरागसेवनोक्तभाग्यकोटिदुष्करं
प्रेमधामदेवमेव नौमि गौरसुन्दरम् ॥५२॥

tyāga-vāhya-bhoga-buddhi-tīvra-daṇḍa-nindanaṁ
rāya-śuddha-kṛṣṇa-kāma-sevanābhi-nandanam
rāya-rāga-sevanokta-bhāgya-koṭi-duskaraṁ
prema-dhāma-devam eva naumi gaurasundaram

TRANSLATION

He strongly condemned those who externally show themselves to be renounced but secretly harbor material desires in their hearts. Yet He praised the untainted confident behavior of the great Vaiṣṇava Rāmānanda Rāya with the *deva-dāsīs* of Śrī Jagannātha Deva, when he taught them the art of dance-drama, as motivated by a pure desire to serve Kṛṣṇa in the mood of *rāga-bhakti*. He further declared that such opportunity as that attained by Rāmānanda to serve the Lord in the *rāga-mārga* is very rare, being the result of millions of births of good fortune. I sing with joy the unending glories of my golden Lord

Gaurasundara the beautiful, the divine abode of pure love.

VERSE 53

श्रीप्रयागभट्टवल्लभैकनिष्ठसेवनं
नीलशैलभट्टदत्तरागमार्गराधनम् ।
श्रीगदाधरार्पिताधिकारमन्त्रमाधुरं
प्रेमधामदेवमेव नौमि गौरसुन्दरम् ॥५३॥

śrī-prayāga-bhaṭṭa-vallabhaika-niṣṭha-sevanaṁ
nīla-śaila-bhaṭṭa-datta-rāga-mārga-rādhanam
śrī-gadādharārpitādhikāra-mantra-mādhuraṁ
prema-dhāma-devam eva naumi gaurasundaram

TRANSLATION

The great Vaiṣṇava *ācārya*, Vallabha Bhaṭṭa (belonging to the province of Andhra) of the *śuddhādvaita sampradāya*, once served the Lord with exclusive, uninterrupted devotion at his house at Prayāga Dhāma. Later on, at Śrī Puruṣottama-kṣetra, the Lord allowed him the priviledge of entering into the conjugal loving service of youthful Kṛṣṇa and arranged for him to learn appropriate scriptural *mantras* under the guidance of Śrī Gadādhara Paṇḍita. I sing with joy the unending glories of my golden Lord Gaurasundara the beautiful, the divine abode of pure love.

VERSE 54

श्रीस्वरूपरायसङ्गगाम्भिरान्त्यलीलनं
द्वादशाब्दवह्निगर्भविप्रलम्भशीलनम् ।
राधिकाधिरूढभावकान्तिकृष्णकुञ्जरं
प्रेमधामदेवमेव नौमि गौरसुन्दरम् ॥५४॥

śrī-svarūpa-rāya-saṅga-gāmbhirāntya-līlanaṁ
dvādaśābda-vahni-garbha-vipralambha-śīlanam
rādhikādhiruḍha-bhāva-kānti-kṛṣṇa-kuñjaraṁ
prema-dhāma-devam eva naumi gaurasundaram

Translation

His pastimes culminated in the *Gambhirā-līlā* with His closest associates Śrī Svarūpa Dāmodara and Śrī Rāmānanda Rāya. For twelve long years He remained within the fire of deep feelings of separation from Kṛṣṇa, which He relished and discussed with His associates. At the same time He was like an elephant, intoxicated with love for Rādhārāṇī, and His being was vibrant with *Rādhā-bhāva*, for He was beautiful Kṛṣṇa Himself illuminated by the beautiful bodily effulgence of Śrī Rādhikā. I sing with joy the unending glories of my golden Lord Gaurasundara the beautiful, the divine abode of pure love.

Verse 55

श्रीस्वरूपकण्ठलग्नमाथुरप्रलापकं
राधिकानुवेदनार्ततीव्रविप्रलम्भकम् ।
स्वप्नवत्समाधिदृष्टदिव्यवर्णनातुरं
प्रेमधामदेवमेव नौमि गौरसुन्दरम् ॥५५॥

śrī-svarūpa-kaṇṭha-lagna-māthura-pralāpakaṁ
rādhikānu-vedanārta-tīvra-vipralambhakam
svapnavat-samādhi-dṛṣṭa-divya-varṇanāturaṁ
prema-dhāma-devam eva naumi gaurasundaram

Translation

Clasping the neck of Śrī Svarūpa Dāmodara, He began to recite sadly the words of lamentation spoken by Śrīmatī Rādhārāṇī when Kṛṣṇa left for Mathurā. He tasted the great pain and desperation experienced by Rādhārāṇī due to intense feelings of separation from Kṛṣṇa. With a heavy heart, the Lord continued to describe realizations which He experienced in absorption of transcendental pastimes, and which are like dreams to outsiders. I sing with joy the unending glories of my golden Lord, Gaurasundara the beautiful, the divine abode of pure love.

Verse 56

सात्त्विकादिभावचिह्नदेहदिव्यसौष्ठवं
कूर्मधर्मभिन्नसन्धिगात्रपुष्पपेलवम् ।
ह्रस्वदीर्घपद्मगन्धरक्तपीतपाण्डुरं
प्रेमधामदेवमेव नौमि गौरसुन्दरम् ॥५६॥

sāttvikādi-bhāva-cihna-deha-divya-sauṣṭhavaṁ
kūrma-dharma-bhinna-sandhi-gātra-puṣpa-pelavam
hrasva-dīrgha-padma-gandha-rakta-pīta-pāṇḍuraṁ
prema-dhāma-devam eva naumi gaurasundaram

Translation

The eight-fold *sāttvika* symptoms of divine love enhance the beauty of His transcendental body. He would sometimes withdraw His limbs into His body like a tortoise, and sometimes His body would become elongated due to His limbs becoming slackened and disjointed. Sometimes His body would be as soft as a flower, and sometimes the color of His body would be red, sometimes yellow, and sometimes it would appear beautified by the pure white hue of the *mallikā* flower. I sing with joy the unending glories of my golden Lord Gaurasundara the beautiful, the divine abode of pure love.

Verse 57

तीव्रविप्रलम्भमुग्धमन्दिराग्रधावितं
कूर्मरूपदिव्यगन्धलुब्धधेनुवेष्टितम् ।
वर्णितालिकूलकृष्णकेलिशैलकन्धरं
प्रेमधाममदेवमेव नौमि गौरसुन्दरम् ॥५७॥

tīvra-vipralambha-mugdha-mandirāgra-dhāvitaṁ
kūrma-rūpa-divya-gandha-lubdha-dhenu-veṣṭitam
varṇitāli-kūla-kṛṣṇa-keli-śaila-kandaraṁ
prema-dhāma-devam eva naumi gaurasundaram

TRANSLATION

Feeling utterly bewildered and grief-stricken, due to intense feelings of separation, He rushed towards the entrance of the temple of Lord Jagannātha. Overcome by great separation, He suddenly fell to the ground, and His body lay there in a contracted form which resembled Kūrma, the tortoise incarnation. He was surrounded by *Telāṅgī* cows who were attracted by the divine fragrance emanating from His body. I sing with joy the unending glories of my golden Lord Gaurasundara the beautiful, the divine abode of pure love.

Verse 58

इन्दुसिन्धुनृत्यदीप्तकृष्णकेलिमोहितं
ऊर्मिशीर्षसुप्तदेहवातरङ्गवाहितम् ।
यामुनालिकृष्णकेलिमग्नसौख्यसागरं
प्रेमधामदेवमेव नौमि गौरसुन्दरम् ॥५८॥

indu-sindhu-nṛtya-dīpta-kṛṣṇa-keli-mohitaṁ
ūrmi-śīrṣa-supta-deha-vāta-raṅga-vāhitam

yāmunāli-kṛṣṇa-keli-magna-saukhya-sāgaraṁ
prema-dhāma-devam eva naumi gaurasundaram

Translation

Once, on a moonlit night, while wandering along the ocean beach with His devotees and tasting the nectar of Kṛṣṇa's pastimes, suddenly He saw the reflection of the moon dancing on the ocean waves. Recollection of the romantic beauty of Śrī Kṛṣṇa's Yamunā pastimes was awakened in His heart, and becoming overwhelmed, He fainted on the spot. In the next instant, unnoticed by others, the Lord's divine form, which seemed to be sleeping (and was rendered light-weight and buoyant like a piece of wood due to His divine ecstatic absorption), was carried away by the breeze in sweet lilting rhythm on the crest of the ocean waves. At that time, He directly saw the transcendental pastimes of Śrī Kṛṣṇa's water sports with the *sakhīs* in the river Kālindī, and He remained merged in the unfathomable ocean of ecstasy. I sing with joy the unending glories of my golden Gaurasundara the beautiful, the divine abode of pure love.

Verse 59

रात्रिशेषसौम्यवेषशायितार्द्रसैकतं
भिन्नसन्धिदीर्घदेहपेलवातिदैवतम् ।
श्रान्तभक्तचक्रतीर्थहृष्टदृष्टिगोचरं
प्रेमधामदेवमेव नौमि गौरसुन्दरम् ॥५९॥

rātri-śeṣa-saumya-veśa-śāyitārdra-saikataṁ
bhinna-sandhi-dīrgha-deha-pelavāti-daivatam
śrānta-bhakta-cakratīrtha-hṛṣṭa-dṛṣṭi-gocaraṁ
prema-dhāma-devam eva naumi gaurasundaram

Translation

Tired after searching for Him throughout the night, the devotees finally found the Lord in the early hours of the morning, lying on the wet sands of Cakra-tīrtha, a figure of tranquility. His divine well-built form, relaxed and sleeping, was elongated, His limbs having become slackened and disjointed. When the devotees thus saw their Lord, their eyes became filled with joy. I sing with joy the unending glories of my golden Lord Gaurasundara the beautiful, the divine abode of pure love.

Verse 60

आर्तभक्तकण्ठकृष्णनामकर्णहृद्गतं
लग्नसन्धिसुष्ठुदेहसर्वपूर्वसंमतम् ।
अर्धवाह्यभावकृष्णकेलिवर्णनातुरं
प्रेमधामदेवमेव नौमि गौरसुन्दरम् ॥६०॥

ārta-bhakta-kaṇṭha-kṛṣṇa-nāma-karṇa-hṛdgataṁ
lagna-sandhi-suṣṭhu-deha-sarva-pūrva-sammatam
ardha-vāhya-bhāva-kṛṣṇa-keli-varṇanāturaṁ
prema-dhāma-devam eva naumi gaurasundaram

Translation

When the anxious devotee's loud chanting of the Holy Name of Kṛṣṇa entered the Lord's ears and touched His heart, His disjointed limbs immediately came together. His previous natural beautiful form appeared, and in half-consciousness, heavy-hearted in the mood of separation, the Lord began to describe various transcendental pastimes of Lord Śrī Kṛṣṇa perceived within His divine absorption. I sing with joy the unending glories of my golden Lord

Gaurasundara the beautiful, the divine abode of pure love.

VERSE 61

यामुनाम्बुकृष्णराधिकालिकेलिमण्डलं
व्यक्तगुप्तदृप्ततृप्तभङ्गिमादनाकुलम् ।
गूढदिव्यमर्ममोदमूर्च्छनाचमत्करं
प्रेमधामदेवमेव नौमि गौरसुन्दरम् ॥६१॥

yāmunānvu-kṛṣṇa-rādhikāli-keli-maṇḍalaṁ
vyakta-gupta-dṛpta-tṛpta-bhaṅgi-mādanākulam
gūṛha-divya-marma-moda-mūrcchanā-camatkaraṁ
prema-dhāma-devam eva naumi gaurasundaram

TRANSLATION

In Śri Vṛndāvana, the different variegated pastimes of Kṛṣṇa with Rādhikā and the *sakhīs* in the waters of the Yamunā charm the heart and mind by many amorous affairs—sometimes manifest, sometimes unseen, sometimes brilliant, sometimes full of loving gestures of contentment. This absolutely charming melody of the heart in the realm of the divine confidential blissful world, which astonishes the whole universe, was distributed by Śrī Caitanya Mahāprabhu. I sing with joy the unending glories of my golden Lord Gaurasundara the beautiful, the divine abode of pure love.

VERSE 62

आस्यघर्षणादिचाटकाद्रिसिन्धुलीलनं
भक्तमर्मभेदितीव्रदुःखसौख्यखेलनम् ।
अत्यचिन्त्यदिव्यवैभवाश्रितैकशङ्करं
प्रेमधामदेवमेव नौमि गौरसुन्दरम् ॥६२॥

āsya-gharṣaṇādi-cāṭakādri-sindhu-līlanaṁ
bhakta-marma-bhedi-tīvra-duḥkha-saukhya-khelanaṁ
atyacintya-divya-vaibhavāśritaika-śaṅkaraṁ
prema-dhāma-devam eva naumi gaurasundaram

TRANSLATION

Upon seeing the Caṭaka mountain, He would rub His lotus face upon the ground in unbearable pain of separation (because by seeing this mountain His memory of Govardhana Hill was aroused), or being reminded of the water sports of Vraja, He would jump into the sea, manifesting the symptoms of divine madness of love. By these divine indications He would transmit desperate waves of pain and pleasure, from the unfathomable depth of the great ocean of transcendental love of Kṛṣṇa, into the hearts of the devotees. I sing with joy the unending glories of my golden Lord Gaurasundara the beautiful, the divine abode of pure love.

VERSE 63

श्रोत्रनेत्रगत्यतीतबोधरोधिताद्भुतं
प्रेमलभ्यभावसिद्धचेतनाचमत्कृतम् ।
ब्रह्मशम्भुवेदतन्त्रमृग्यसत्यसुन्दरं
प्रेमधामदेवमेव नौमि गौरसुन्दरम् ॥६३॥

śrotra-netra-gatyatīta-bodha-rodhitādbhutaṁ
prema-labhya-bhāva-siddha-cetanā-camatkṛtam
brahma-śambhu-veda-tantra-mṛgya-satya-sundaraṁ
prema-dhāma-devam eva naumi gaurasundaram

Translation

Lord Gaurāṅga is beyond the purview of the power of sight and hearing, and stuns the advances of the intellect. He astounds even those whose hearts are firmly self-controlled, overwhelming them with love. Even in the case of Lord Brahmā and Lord Śiva, the Vedic and Tantric scriptures which are revealed by them are simply searching after the Supreme Lord. I sing with joy the unending glories of my golden Lord Gaurasundara the beautiful, the divine abode of pure love.

Verse 64

विप्रशूद्रविज्ञमूर्खयावनादिनामदं
बिहृविक्रमोच्चनीचसज्जनैकसम्पदम् ।
स्त्रीपुमादिनिर्विवादसार्ववादिकोद्धरं
प्रेमधामदेवमेव नौमि गौरसुन्दरम् ॥६४॥

vipra-śudra-vijña-mūrkha-yāvanādi-nāmadaṁ
vitta-vikramocca-nīca-sajjanaika-sampadam
strī-pumādi-nirvivāda-sārvavādikoddharaṁ
prema-dhāma-devam eva naumi gaurasundaram

Translation

He has purified the *brāhmaṇa* and the *śūdra*, the scholar and the fool, and even the *yāvana* and other *non-āryans*. He is the super-excellent opulence possessed by all gentle and sincere souls, both rich and poor, high-born and low-born. He is unanimously accepted by all as the savior of all beings, in both the mundane and spiritual world, irrespective of male or female. I sing with joy the unending glories of my golden Lord Gaurasundara the beautiful, the divine abode of pure love.

VERSE 65

सिन्धुशून्यवेदचन्द्रशाककुम्भपूर्णिमा
सान्ध्यचान्द्रकोपरागजातगौरचन्द्रमा ।
स्नानदानकृष्णनामसङ्गतत्परात्परं
प्रेमधामदेवमेव नौमि गौरसुन्दरम् ॥६५॥

sindhu-śūnya-veda-candra-śāka-kumbha-pūrṇimā
sāndhya-cāndrakoparāga-jāta-gaura-candramā
snāna-dāna-kṛṣṇa-nāma-saṅga-tat-parātparaṁ
prema-dhāma-devam eva naumi gaurasundaram

TRANSLATION

In the year 1407 Śākābda, in the month of Phālguṇa, on the evening of the full moon and at the onset of the lunar eclipse, the Supreme Absolute Truth, Śrī Gauracandra, appeared like the moon. Joy abounded in the hearts of all. Many bountiful presentations of jewels and other valuables were offered to the Lord and charity was generously distributed in all directions; countless masses bathed in the holy waters of the Gaṅgā, and above all, there was the loud congregational chanting of the Holy Names of Kṛṣṇa (*hari-nāma saṅkīrtana*). I sing with joy the unending glories of my golden Lord Gaurasundara the beautiful, the divine abode of pure love.

VERSE 66

आत्मसिद्धसावलीलपूर्णसौख्यलक्षणं
स्वानुभावमत्तनृत्यकीर्त्तनात्मवण्टनम् ।

अद्वयैकलक्ष्यपूर्णतत्त्वतत्परात्परं
प्रेमधामदेवमेव नौमि गौरसुन्दरम् ॥६६॥

ātma-siddha-sāvalīla-pūrṇa-saukhya-lakṣaṇaṁ
svānubhāva-matta-nṛtya-kīrtanātma-vanṭanam
advayaika-lakṣya-pūrṇa-tattva-tat-parātparaṁ
prema-dhāma-devam eva naumi gaurasundaram

TRANSLATION

He is the source of self-evident perfect bliss which is full of natural loving pastimes. His dancing (*nṛtya*) arises from the intoxication of overflowing spiritual bliss, and His chanting of the Holy Name and fame of the Supreme Lord (*kīrtana*) arises from the attempt to enjoy and distribute that spiritual bliss. These two characteristics are the two natural and fundamental substantial symptoms of the perfect absolute principle. Therefore He is *asamordhva*—no one can equal or surpass Him, for He is the unalloyed Supreme Truth. I sing with joy the unending glories of my golden Lord Gaurasundara the beautiful, the divine abode of pure love.

VERSE 67

श्रीपुरीश्वरानुकम्पिलब्धदीक्षदैवतं
केशवाख्यभारतीसकाशकेशरक्षितम् ।
माधवानुधीकिशोरकृष्णसेवनादरं
प्रेमधामदेवमेव नौमि गौरसुन्दरम् ॥६७॥

śrī-purīśvarānukampi-labdha-dīkṣa-daivataṁ
keśavākhya-bhāratī-sakāśa-keśa-rakṣitam
mādhavānudhī-kiśora-kṛṣṇa-sevanādaraṁ
prema-dhāma-devam eva naumi gaurasundaram

TRANSLATION

He blessed Śrī Īśvara Purī and expressed His mercy by accepting initiation from him. He accepted the dress of the renounced order, *sannyāsa*, from Keśava Bhāratī, shaving off His beautiful long hair. He adored pure loving service in the conjugal mood to Śrī Kiśora Kṛṣṇa, which was displayed by Mādhavendra Purī, considering this service to be the most elevated. I sing with joy the unending glories of my golden Gaurasundara the beautiful, the divine abode of pure love.

VERSE 68

सिन्धुविन्दुवेदचन्द्रशाकफाल्गुणोदितं
न्याससोमनेत्रवेदचन्द्रशाकबोधितम् ।
वाणवाणवेदचन्द्रशाकलोचनान्तरं
प्रेमधामदेवमेव नौमि गौरसुन्दरम् ॥६८॥

sindhu-vindu-veda-candra-śāka-phālgunoditaṁ
nyāsa-soma-netra-veda-candra-śāka-bodhitam
vāṇa-vāṇa-veda-candra-śāka-locanātaraṁ
prema-dhāma-devam eva naumi gaurasundaram

TRANSLATION

Like the moon, the golden Lord Gaurasundara rose in the sky of Gauḍa (Śrī Māyāpura) in the year 1407 Śākābda. He displayed His pastimes of accepting *sannyāsa* in the year 1431 Śākābda and He disappeared from this world in the year 1455 Śākābda. I sing with joy the unending glories of my golden Gaurasundara the beautiful, the divine abode of pure love.

VERSE 69

श्रीस्वरूपरायसङ्गहर्षशेषघोषणं
शिक्षणाष्टकाख्यकृष्णकीर्त्तनैकपोषणम् ।
प्रेमनाममात्रविश्वजीवनैकसम्भरं
प्रेमधामदेवमेव नौमि गौरसुन्दरम् ॥६९॥

śrī-svarūpa-rāya-saṅga-harṣa-śeṣa-ghoṣanaṁ
śikṣanāṣṭakākhya-kṛṣṇa-kīrtanaika-poṣaṇam
prema-nāma-mātra-viśva-jīvanaika-sambharaṁ
prema-dhāma-devam eva naumi gaurasundaram

TRANSLATION

With ecstatic joy, He told his closest and dearmost associates Śrī Svarūpa Dāmodara and Śrī Rāmānanda Rāya that *Kṛṣṇa-nāma saṅkīrtana* is supremely beneficial for the living entities of Kali-yuga: '*harṣe prabhu kahe śuna svarūpa rāma rāya, nāma saṅkīrtana kalu parama upāya.*' In his famous *Śikṣāṣṭaka* He gave Śrī Kṛṣṇa *saṅkīrtana* the highest place above all, and He conclusively taught that the chanting of Kṛṣṇa`s Holy Names with devotion is the only means of support and sustenance of every living being within the universe. I sing with joy the unending glories of my golden Gaurasundara the beautiful, the divine abode of pure love.

VERSE 70

प्रेमहेमदेव देहि दासरेशमान्यतां
क्षम्यतां महापराधराशिरेष गण्यताम् ।
रूपकिङ्करेषु रामानन्ददाससम्भरं
प्रेमधामदेवमेव नौमि गौरसुन्दरम् ॥७०॥

prema hema-deva dehi-dāsareṣa-manyatāṁ
kṣamyatāṁ mahāparādha-rāśireṣa-gaṇyatām
rūpa-kiṅkareṣu rāmānanda dāsa-sambharaṁ
prema-dhāma-devam eva naumi gaurasundaram

TRANSLATION

O my golden Lord! O ocean of love! Please bestow Your treasure of love. Please give a little attention to this fallen soul and forgive his countless offenses. Please look upon him as one of the servants of Thy closest and dearmost servant, Śrī Rūpa. O Lord, You are the only sustainer and bestower of fortune upon this Rāmānanda Dāsa. All glories, all glories, all glories unto You, my golden Lord of divine love, Gaurasundara the beautiful. I sing forever Your unending glories.

VERSE 71

सश्रद्धदः सप्तदशकं प्रेमधामेति नामकम् ।
स्तवं कोऽपि पठन् गौरं राधाश्याममयं व्रजेत् ॥७१॥

saśraddhaḥ-sapta-daśakaṁ-prema-dhāmeti-nāmakaṁ
stavaṁ ko'pi paṭhan gauraṁ rādhāśyāmamayaṁ vrajet

TRANSLATION

He who studies, recites, or sings with regard, faith, and devotion these seventy verses by the name of *Prema-Dhāma-Deva-Stotram* will obtain the loving devotional service of Śrī Gaurasundara, who is Śyāmasundara Himself, resplendent in the mood and luster of Śrīmatī Rādhārāṇī.

VERSE 72

पञ्चमे शतगौराब्दे श्रीसिद्धान्तसरस्वती ।
श्रीधरः कोऽपि तच्छिष्यस्त्रिदण्डी नौति सुन्दरम् ॥७२॥

pañcame śata gaurābde-śrī-siddhānta-sarasvatī
śrīdharaḥ ko'pi tacchiṣyastridaṇḍī-nauti-sundaram

TRANSLATION

This *stotram* has been composed in the year 500 Gaurābda by a *tridaṇḍī* disciple of Śrī Siddhānta Sarasvatī by the name of Śrīdhara.

OTHER TITLES
BY SWAMI B. R. SRIDHARA

books

The Search for Śrī Kṛṣṇa: Reality the Beautiful
Śrī Guru and His Grace
The Golden Volcano of Divine Love
The Hidden Treasure of the Sweet Absolute
Kīrtana Mañjuṣā
Loving Search for the Lost Servant
Subjective Evolution
Śrī Śrī Prapanna Jīvanāmṛtam
Sermons From the Guardian of Devotion, Vol. 1,2
Bhajana Madhuri
Follow the Angels

small books

The Guardian of Devotion
Sermons From the Guardian of Devotion, Vol. 3,4
Ambrosia in the Lives of Surrendered Souls
Golden Staircase
Home Comfort
Inner Fulfillment
Heart and Halo
Holy Engagement
Absolute Harmony

videos

Absolute Harmony
Śrī Gāyatrī